Lobe Scarps & Finials

Geraldine Monk

- Leafe Press -

Published by Leafe Press

4 Cohen Close
Chilwell
Nottingham
NG9 6RW
United Kingdom

1864 Morgan Avenue
Claremont, California 91711
United States

www.leafepress.com

Cover image © 2011 by Alan Halsey

A catalogue record for this book is available from the British Library

ISBN 978-0-9561919-4-6

Contents

Glow in the Darklunar Calendar 5

Print & Pin 27

A Nocturnall Upon S. Lucies Day 41

Poppyheads 49

Three Fathoms

    All My Sea 59
    The Wrong Boat 63
    Other Constellations Look 66

Raccoon

    Part One: Dreams in Absentia 69
    Part Two: Stella's Dream 85

Just Another Day 101

Acknowledgements 105

Glow in the Darklunar Calendar

January

Two Thousand and Ten again.
I suppose it's time we apologised to
Mr & Mrs Neanderthal for
dashing out their yam noodles against
their last cave of
pots and lip gloss.
I never for a minute thought
they were Millwall fans.

Old Moon

To wake so early on the
New Year with wings
skimming massive
move of dream retreats
through slits of
eyelids.
What on earth?

Moon After Yule

Hey! Archaeopteryx.
Urvogel.
What on earth in heaven's
name are you doing here in
my inner city window?

Ice Moon

The owl disappeared itself hours ago
down the warped gullet of a
dreary decade.
Minerva smiling into space.
The first bird lost its
flock.

Wolf Moon

The supernatural is full on and fierce.

Like little tongues
snowflakes lap the
cheek of my first barefaced
sentences of the decade and the
first death came before the first melting.

Moon of the Terrible

Funerals flood us with ourselves
our memory is now all of you.
In my best mute face I scry the
secret recipe for hedgehog pasties
buried for ever under a glorious

sky   *Cooking Moon*

falling between and apart
stretch of clouded ligaments
longing the throat to wail an
aria as good as a
wolf but
twice as
foxy

                                    Quiet Moon

all in a moonless month
full of fabulous birds and their absence.

February

starts with an animal
swim – paddling paws

Raccoon Moon

hot breath crosses
bristle of chlorine a soft a
real soft slash of cherry reddens
turquoise at either side the
deep continental
drift casts a bad eclipse on
municipal glass
ceiling

Snow Moon

slate blue pigeons
block gutters
fat collared doves
block gutters
one sorry magpie
blocks gutters

Storm Moon

spring plays peek-a
droll with deathly
I fold away the paper – the
details were so very grim
(we always let our beauty down)

Hunger Moon

a leaping month on deep lows
what a pantomime –
loneliness inside the
February wardrobe palpitates

Candles Moon

March

^hup^hup^hup^hup^
  rough month ready
     bad boy
^hup^hup^hup^hup^

Lion. Yes you! You're on.
Come on in nithering
rampant rump ball
sockets sunk in a
wall of florid teeth
withering arctic.
Lambkins dithering in wings.

Moon of Winds and Sore Eyes

Beware ides
tides and
rip cavings.
My white lucent
wine trembles with
unstable cut of
solid
gas. glory. be.

Sleep Moon

Rock runs to slurry.
Earthquakes cakewalk the
globe and back.

dunder. earth. death. dearth. abide.

Crust Moon

The whole of
South America
moves west
within minutes
maps antiquate.

Families search family.

Lenten Moon

Better to be
born granite-faced than
marrow-boned. Two a penny
catastrophes
wreath of heart-broke
wreathed with lovelorn.

Chaste Death Moon

Half-mad-half-mud
loon-calf-fond face
steaming.

Sugar Sap Moon

Blair makes prayers
&
mansion millions.

Worm Moon

O.K. lamb –
meek it out …

April

*'They may have a slight
yellowing of the foliage or
look a little drawn.
This is quite natural after
travelling in a dark box'*

as plants as humans
no matter – we are all – so very banana

Sprouting Grass Moon

April is the fool of months
showers and politics all
the rage of all
the tired people
force-fed and fed-up

Pink & Full Fish Moon

crumpled mask bakes ...
we boil our morning
bread and water our faces

Waking & Seed & Full Egg Moon

supernatural quick fix
outstrips demand
flowering onions downed with
snake oil optimism

Red Grass Appearing Moon

volcanic ash paves a fright of
sheer craftless skyways –
birds wing their atavistic myth
fresh of flesh & wimberry-eyed

Wild Cat Moon

Mind the celestial gap.

May

sidling to Byzantium

Milk Moon

exact positioning:
trinity of
blue:
mosque
water
sky

Planting Moon

above the Judas Tree
we watch the *Irish Sea*
slide into the
Bosphorus

Flower Moon

floaters play eyetricks
horizons rising eating
Noah's pudding
drinking sweet milkless tea

Hare's moon

Lepus. Formations. The angels of
Chora with six wings bite. Hold that
judder on that thought:
biting angels with
angry teeth
(teeth?)

Dragon Moon

biting night wind brings
half god of inexhaustible power

mistress of life and wild nature

Mothers Moon

in the abstraction of face
rose madder genuine shakes a
fugitive hue of matter fixed with
a deep roving

Frogs Returning Moon

Byzantium *was* the month of May
the rest was back
home for a coalition
night of a thousand cuts
banks rolling
pin money through
all our bright
tomorrow's bread

Corn Moon

a golden sovereign hanging by a
thread

June

love
love lies
love lies bleeding

Lotus Moon

futile massacre
crushed the sun
hypoxic rogue doing a
dead zone
coast

Strong Sun Moon

packed up the month of short nights
stacked with noctilucent whispers

Rose Moon

out the blue came
another blue
nest of celestial dolls
soft suede shout

Strawberry Moon

global embalming
cool temple silk
worms
doing a
here we go
mulberry

Mimosa Moon

here we go

Moon of Horses

July

spurge.   glory lily.   loose strife.
another fine mess:
rain rained on the parade
slaters disembowelled baby
tomatoes
spuds sodden to misery

Mead Moon

and to cry about
one more guy with a gun
peppering the news with ruined
lives

Moon of Claiming

floods & blasts & the world over
is in a fit of bad temper
crabbed with interference from
invisible sun spots

Thunder Moon

everything was hurting
with artificial colouring and
quantitative faking

Full Buck Moon

so sailing to Greenwich at full noon
on a wet dark day in a bright
good mood the world was replaced by
a multitude of women
reaching one crescendo

Hungry Ghost Moon

August

It began well – celestial trumpeters
promising dazzlement – aurora alerts
as far south as Derbyshire.
Then it flopped bad-eggish
from nothing came nowt – the
solar max threw a wobbler –
everything was elsewhere and
being England it was cloudy.

Dog Days Moon

So it goes. As per usual. Silly season.
Serpiente de verano.
Rain peppered burnt sausages.
Emulsified chorizo. Salmonella mayo.

Corn Moon

Colder. Wetter.
Perseids a proper shower
hurtling a best-in-years
outta-sight and
being England it was cloudy.

Dispute Moon

The Peaks
tucked up its
moorlands.
In the unseeing
tidy of dark
breeze upon breeze
rocks outcrops of city
cars into cradles.

Women's Moon

Out here
Dove
is not a
bird but a
burr
of
Dark Water.

Moon When All Things Ripen

Out here
heather
crinkles a-lectric.

Lightening Moon

September

All the women slept
as the band played on
a night out curled into
mass catnap
forming
puddles of
Lethe.

Singing Moon

Jupiter in benign
opposition
luminous as a water
chestnut.
We are all atomic children
of catastrophic stardust.

Chrysanthemum Moon

Sensible flowers of
mourning &
lamentation. Brash asteroid
faces. Symmetrical petals
facing a
weakening sun.

Harvest Moon

Shine on!
The extinct ghost orchid
is
so not again but always
was
nondescript
with
unseen unsung.

When Calves Grow Hair Moon

Mercury rising

Nut Moon

Venus rising

Mulberry Moon

In the overheated
hotel room
feet swell the
smell of suet
pudding drifts from
canteen desiccation

Ripe Moon

eyes barb on a smear of
view through caked
panes we scraped a
fabrication
snatching
cool of
clean-cut
deep.

Black Butterfly Moon

October

Full of America and wild rice.

Windermanoth Moon

In their fall came our
summer
lapping up our
continental
shift

Kindly Moon

sun dose
soak of vitamins
hug hug hug
boulder dog
inner-sprung
deep earth
plumb

Hunter's Moon

transit of Idaho high
passes of uncuttable
moose tongue
tales of unspeakable
childish butchery
ran rivers of red
ran scarlet ribbons

Blood Moon Falling

liver shanks gut yarns
English Longbow her
chosen trajectory

Long Hair Moon

Harriet Lake to Black Hawk
Island via Dreamtime dark
matters lighten cryogenic
cha-cha-cha

      Shedding Moon

leaping feathers

          Wine Moon

leopard frogs

             Travel Moon

infestation of glory vision
crossing La Crosse to
Minnesota ascending Highway 61
in Michael's mid-life Chrysler

                  Vintage Moon

the Mississippi stretched
a lump in the throat out and

                      Blackberry Moon

out and out and out

                        Winterfelleth Moon

and out and out and out

November

Absorbing another
rare earth-like planet
discovered at the
world's end of the
Goldilocks
zone.

Fledgling Raptor Moon

Absorbing another
rare earth-like planet
discovered at the
world's end of the
Goldilocks
zone.

Freezing River Moon

Rumblings of croque
celestial crisis : La Luna is
shrinking. If struck it
would sound like a bell.

Mad Moon

Boulder-boffins consult
lobate scarps measuring
shadows and craters of
belittlement.

Dark Moon

Distraction of predictions
solar maximus trumpets
world with end halleluiah
Armageddon party.

Poverty Moon

With windings and
endings and
shrinkings
and shrieking.

Deer Rutting Moon

Lost dances of
earthly delights
repeat and delete
perpetual repetition
repertoire repertoire.

Fog Moon

Is that really the time?

All Gathered Moon

Vegetables must be
peeled eyes removed
hearts recovered. Fruit flesh
parted with gravity.

Trading Moon

Tonguing the nebulous
taste and almost-colour of
Palma Violets it seems extra
ordinary that the universe is beige.

Horns Broken Off Moon

December

Distracted by a big snow
a new moon positioned in an
exhibition over the Don Valley.

Small Spirits Moon

Anti-twilight skews
expectation of night – the
Belt of Venus daubed
outskirts of Earth casting
its shadow across
its own horizon.

Long Night Moon

Super soft-focussed Rotho.

Under Burn Moon

Out the car radio a meteor
as massive as the clock
face in our car boot heads
earthwards. Weirdly
growing weary of doomsday.
What time is it Mr Wolf?

Oak Moon

Out of Heathrow:
Skirmishes over yoga mats!
Random Airlines grounded!
Bless you snow. Birds wing their
atavistic myth once more
fresh of flesh & wimberry-eyed.

Bitter Moon

Janus is coming
two-faced and getting
fat with nerves. Pipes
burst out with tension
ringing in the midnight
plumbers change to gold dust.

Little Finger Moon

Glass slippers & night scented
frocks waft towards the city
lights. From the yellowing
festive tree the stuffed
snowy owl plays at being
scary ghost bird and succeeds.

Cold Time Moon

Minerva smiling into space.

Frost Fish Moon

This year's end ends with
ominous lunar eclipse
falling on an ominous
winter solstice. It passed
without event so far as we could
see the coast was clear.

Ashes Fire Moon

What say you Janus? What do you see?
What will be will be on the eve of another
year I suppose it's time we apologised to
Mr & Mrs Neanderthal whilst we can.

Twelfth Moon

Print & Pin

To Stout Trees Gently

LOST

In
space
between

knave
&
queen

blue tune whistling up a
wind-up

clockwork hackles
crimped
full sore
with
snoutish
beat

it flew out my hands
wending

little-piggy-like

awayway

home-longing

mulch loved
hand hot
as
felled leaves

FOUND

A loaf of
rawbush

shape of a chopwreck
rye & emotional

weeps

all day

in the heart of our

garden

sorely with

sour cries of

wishlorn

(have grown attached)

would like for it a
goodish
bush home
with happy
curtains

LOST

my soul

upon a time

flew out the window

at twilight

searching for a search party

a dog-eared tag of a soul

are you with me?
come closer
closer still
(oops mind the doo)

I smell your breath – thank you

colourless is my
brave now
world

without it and in
a dread sea mist amid
encircling
gloom

answers to
Wagtail
with or without wing

FOUND

beneath a tzeeping-drip

SUSH

a flock of half-baked

l-o-n-g-t-h-o-u-g-h-t-s

colour of uncooked ham-hock

slightly needy

)on verge of a nervous breakweep(

could be

blubbish

(responds to that name)

– unwanted gaff –

FREE CORRECTION

TEL.

OOOOOOOOOOOOOOOOOOOOOO

LOST

much loved
I
dentity
answered to
A
name
aka
hypocoristic

missed much at weekends
absconded on
Monday morning

(((((((((((on reflection
it was reflection
was
a mirage))))))))))

it started in a
fish-shaped bottle
full of herbs and olive oil
(what's that all about?)

meet me at the next tree but one

bring your own mirror

desperately
peaky

FOUND

cawing kittens

in

golden fleece tree

unwanted excitation

bloody flux-a-churning

seven or more maws

x-teasel claws

tin-tin

unravelling peace

wild bird-cat strike

doth-do

deathly stuff

fort

fun

pluck 'em clean

can deliver

LOST

A broken earring

cheap & tearful

sentimental value

last seen between
disappointments

nervous fingers
crushed its fraught gallery

frags with squibs
my darling

would we be strangers

untied

pretty lobe of the year reward

for your esteemed

shell-like

contact

Looby of the Long Hair
third dear red door from
this near miss

FOUND

Sweet Nothings

Saturday morning

behind wheelie bins

wet through with clownish

responds to any fond name

changes colour with rude

manners

strange teeth

only one ear

bit of a mouthful

love

might come of it

might

not

contact the back of
this petrified
frond

LOST

A link of words

terribly

well connected with

vellum

embarrassingly personal

last seen breaking

across an anger

owner

deeply winded

blind-baking

short crusty finger things

for third parties

please approach with

utter

may nibble

can collect

FOUND

footfall

unhumanlike

lying at midnight

under our doormat

pulsates in

goonlight

taps a toe in

lukewarm & foppish

would love to rather

get rid of

free to first
comer
please
hurry
please
no
bogus
callers
or
distressed linen

LOST

Hecate

also answers to

Trivia

spooky moon spectre

apes

good-goddess

last seen at three-pronged
crossroads
in
Nether Edge

if found please
don't feed her
dog head
snake head
horse head
nor her ghost hounds

leave a message on this
stump
and
scoot
crazy for your life
to
unbendy path place

A Nocturnall Upon S. Lucies Day
Being The Shortest Day

A Collaboration with John Donne

For
Chris Goode
13th December

This end is your beginning

Tis the yeares midnight,
                    it is the dayes, Lucies,
who scarce seaven
                    hours
herself unmaskes.

So place Iraq
ever-so-gently
into a state of
pending
wrap it fast in
swaddling clothes
tie a tinsel tag
around
its sore and sorry toe –
                    let it go
for the worlds all
sap is sunke:

    The generall balme
    th'hydroptique earth
    hath drunk,
    whither, as to
    the beds-feet,
    life is shrunke,
    dead and enterr'd;

laugh at

                    we their

                              Epitaph

bee spring thing
new alchimie
expresse
nothingness
emptiness
re-begot
          not
       are not
     which are not
  things which are not
you me s/he re-begot
            not
again
    of absence
dearth   of
       things
   not
no
    things
      not

lovers
    be
lovers
    be
next
    be
dead
    be
next

every dead thing
dull privations
leane
  on meanboned
beauty be bountyfling
ruin'd
   art
expressed
a quintessence even
from
no
things which are *not*
which are *not*
are *not*
things
no
    thingness
no
  thingness

no rest to wrest
rest to wrest
to wrest
wrest
-est
-st
-t

Lucie   Loves   Lucifer
Darkkinglux   **Hates**   **Queenb**lindlight
lights fight to the death
of life
which light will win
the dish
brimming with eyes

before

drawn-out-dawn

four candles play the vigil
on a precipice of hair

white-big big-frocked
red
sasht
saffron buns abreast
all the sons
y-e-s
go
the
Star Boys
pointy hats erect

The lesser sun shines
goat-runne-fetch
new-lust

the body must
         be
here body
         be
must
    be
here
   be
body must
     be
the body must
        be

        as shadow

   if we an ordinary
   nothing
were

an echo caught
     in looped
       light

        prepare towards
       the yeares dayes deep
         midnight

        is

Poppyheads

Since 937 AD a church has stood on the spot which is occupied by The Minster Church of Rotherham All Saints in South Yorkshire. It has been a minster since the 15th Century. Pevsner said it was 'the best perpendicular church in the country'.

When I first entered the interior a dark gloomy day became even darker. The minster was ill-lit and virtually empty. Heaven.

That day I found three special things to take away: a stash of red-skinned windfall apples to be had for a donation, the tender name of Goodeth and the wondrous discovery of the term poppyhead.

Poppyhead describes the carved finials that adorn the end of church pews or stalls. Some are in the form of the fleur-de-lys, fruit and foliage, others are exquisite scrawlings of strange animal or humanoid creatures. It is thought poppyhead derives from the French poupée meaning doll or puppet.

I
float
to the
edge of my pond –
flutters bug me. Litter. Water louse.
Damsels in. Nothing is for ever. Floozies
ply. So long dragons – fly now nymphs.

It was like the Marie Celeste except
we weren't at sea and no one was missing.
In a late summer night courtyard illuminated
shafts of wet creaked a simmering up-deep.

I
walk
to the
edge of my pond –
heavy base diameter
harsh on wayward circumference.
Oxygenators raid aquatic glad-cake.

How greener is the other side of the
body incorruptible?
Kiss un-pouting glass. Cold soars.
Eternal life is everlasting pants.

I
lope
to the
edge of my pond –
the bulk of my me-body teeters
brink-blessed rump askew
inglenook on the outer warming

♣

One serpent short of Eden
the garden warbles in excelsior. Weeding
pesky Latin names I grow bonnets
slippers & ladies ear-drops. Hock-hock.

♣

I
prod
the
edge of my pond –
tips on my toes urging reflection.
Outriders all in a row Mr Water
Boatman all thumbs upping.

♣

Moderation didn't make the
universe burst into pentameters.
Extremes teem. Petals and
thorns. Throne of frowns.

I
stalk
to the
edge of my pond –
trembling like a leaflet. Greenhorn twig.
Trotting fingers mince a dance.
Stance soft hewn with feelers.

Dissembling blossoms
getting their peckers up for
autumnal crumble. Plum duff happens.
Lackadaisical bees – get well soon.

I
balk
at the
edge of my pond –
there we go – there us goes again
slatters of déjà vu
ur-nouns re-occurring.

Swung my lungs out –
the first tomato has ripened.
I breath spoonfuls of ethylene joy.
What measure a semi hemidemisemiquaver!

I
flitter
to the
edge of my pond –
yield of utter words. Black &
bleeding Decker strimdrop. Lop dry
your drone-drone. Up it and phut shut.

♣

Object awaiting narratives.
Doll head shot the plot – plaited fog.
Eggcups preened with weirdness.
Scary too that little chair – legs up in the airless.

♣

I
shimmy
to the
edge of my pond –
a long swagger on small water is
under construction. Street cred newts
lock-popping with hydro-boogaloos.

♣

The sun doesn't always
rise – it always can't always be not
tomorrow determined by rain & the
North Sea ferry with its loud lavatories.

I
quake
at the
edge of my pond –
the terribly nice age iced over.
Eye motes congregate. A murder of
crows flock. Other birds flew blightfully.

Little toes: unsung gems twitch a
ceaseless uppish. Pivotal antennae.
Ballistic ballet lobs an arabesque
from haunch to crenellation.

I
slept
on the
edge of my pond –
a storm with attitude drawled an
alien accent. Music for a while …
shrinking violent hymnal.

Be careful what you wish for.
Runny eggs on sunny bread can
cast a trickle. A brutal door is not a
feather misheard in an ill wind.

Three Fathoms

All My Sea

liverwinds
        kindazzle
up
    my coastal dreams –
grossgrog
      bulkram
           bustywater

the sea and other animals
should not be teased

      your mid feather
      your oyster egg

wrackwinds
       bladder
up
    my central city soul –
mournfly
     melancholic
         memoir

besides the
      I do sea
a childflood
   of olive oil
     love
slapped on
     barefaced paddles
lapping mid Fifties fall out

Windscale
     leaks radioact
up
   pepperminted rock
       pool
written all the way through
        illuminations
glowered in the dark

extreme sentimentality
the trump card of capitalists

to be born without
the shipping forecast
spelting
through my
mid-ship-mind
shadowing deep
death at dinner time
and tea
is to be only
half born

      your mid exquisite wave
      your ovulating crest

lost in sandmares

          wonderworld sees worryworld
               in a grain

The Wrong Boat

Traversing the Tagus
in a totally wrong
     rose
steeped in hermetically sealed
  Pyrex
without dishiness or sails
without
    bumpz and liltz

riding in the back of an infernal Sea Cat

cooped up
and close
wi
Nick Cave &
K. Minogue
(tiny little thing)
in yer face
blasting faulty
  murther
    ballads

we blank-eyed the wet proof
video water
beyond the doubled-glazed glass
shell

  our withering was a
system without weather
  caught in a one way ticket
across the premature Styx

   d-d-d-d-d-dey-call
   d-d-d-d-d-dey—call
   dddd
   m-me ddd

the skin on our skin
turning sardine
sans silver
gathering
smell without
sea
or
sin

d-d-d-dwild
d-d-d-dewild

murderous to the soul
is a faulty sound
system trapped
in a trapped space

rrrrrrrrrooooosssssseee

murderous to women &
giggly girls
are faulty men
in a trapped excuse

they call me the wild rose
but my name is just my name

cor de rosa

her lips were the colour of roses

bacalhau
cor de rosa
stains the sky
cor de rosa
bacalhau

they call me the wild rose

cod ballads

where the wild
roses grow

between
her
name is
      just her name
between her

cor de rosa

        we kissed goodbye
        all beauty must die
        on the last day

between her
her
between
her
rosa

cor de rosa

drowning teeth

and

fins

Other Constellations Look

behind *light* seeps *behind* light *seeps* behind *ligh*
t seeps *behind* light *seeps* behind *light* seeps beh

       burnt at stake
                      burnt steak
      jinxed high
             jacket
                  smells brickish
    no human   no scarf   warmth

-light-creeps-behind-light-creeps-behind-light-
-creeps-behind-light-creeps-behind-light-creeps-

      saddle sored
                     lifer
          love lost lips
                      detritus
    no scarf crashes   harm
                    jacket hums

(weeps)(behind)(light)(weeps)(behind)(light)(weeps)
(behind)(light)(weeps)(behind)(light)(weeps)(behind)

    permanent deflection
                  cramps
         remembrance
                 all is maybe room
   jacket stills stock   absence
             alarms
    no human   no comforter

(((((((((behindlightseepscreepsweepsbe)))))))))

Raccoon

For Laura and Nick

Part One

Dreams In Absentia

'All the yard-arms were tipped with a pallid fire; and touched at each tri-pointed lightning-rod-end with three tapering white flames, each of the three tall masts was silently burning in that sulphurous air, like three gigantic wax tapers before an altar.'

Herman Melville, *Moby Dick*

But
(whatever possessed him moved him)

as
I
packed crosswords
he
packed Moby
and the rest was
this-story

.
.
.
.
.
.
.
.
.
.
.
.
.
.
.
.

Watching The Weather Channel in San Francisco
(bouts of light flirt through blinds)

... what's that she said?
            forthcoming from the
bosom she heaved
                        'a bountiful gulf moisture'
spreading from the south
        yea upward
curving
            munificence

lotion unleashed in the headwind
            drifting slowly
to the four corners of my toilet bag

there she blows

here we blew

too northerly
     too westerly
          to feel the bounty brush ...

... what's that beneath my finger?

Lowly, longly a wail went forth ...

Never Seeing Whales
(schools of rocks moved)

Walking beyond walking
distance without
a car
is how hard we tried
to see you:
we tried so hard
we saw
outcrops of
rocks
move
and
hump
and
spout
and
even if they weren't whales
we sure damn got excited
about the rocks
moving
and
in
the low-glowing
retrospect
of disappointment
rocks moving is
even
more amazing
than whales
moving
even
if the rocks
didn't
really move

But Out the Blue Poolside Up
(not seeking sprouts a vision)

Lo!

h

u

m

m

i

n

g

b

i

r

d

!　　!

And

don't

blink

oh

ye

eyes

of

mine

be

on

hold!

Celestial Grammar
(suck it and see)

When a world holds itself.

Oh periwinkle!

I cannot describe that
old moon
in the new moon's arms
in Idaho

in rare desert air hung
a savage punctuation
in a too big sky
to dislodge from
my retina
a souvenir of speech.

Oh drupaceous damson!

But When Word Crew Jumps Ship
(doom-plummet of the heavenly orb)

New research:
new moons and full
relax and squeeze
seas
relax and squeeze
rocks
relax and squeeze
radon
killing us humans
disheartening our proverbs
ladling our dreams with doom
confounding our every last romantic.

Is there nothing sacred that is not out to kill us?

Oh pass the
lethal sea salt for my
deadly red meat
ye murderous oceans!

Never Seeing Elk
(I eat your tender girder)

I looked everywhere:
        on that rare fillet of Point Reyes
        along the San Andreas Fault
        in EverwetEvergreen
        in clandestine skirting boards
        under unpressurized skies
        in the cymbal-clash of hand palm
        under palm-crash of tree leaves
        in a sheaf of Alan's hair
        straggling white Egyptian
        cotton sheets
        in shadowesque
        frettings
        in netted clouds
        clotted lace curtains
        in the patina of
        Mrs Dash
        scattered picante
        in pottage
        and the whole
        coast road from
        San Fran
        to
        Near Death:
Nada

But Something Nighed in Boise
(Cathy puts a pot roast on – we all have tea)

Amidships the veg
was
a three letter word
beginning with
'E'
getting low
down & dirty with
laughing stock
I spy the irony
with both little
eyes staring back at
me
grunting from
the bathroom
mirror a
forest echo
of dewlap
& antlers.

I pack three pine cones
deep in bubblewrap.

Never seeing Mount Rainier
(we strain my eyes with cloudburst)

'But that's not a mountain!'
smiles Zoë gorgeously aslant
driving with her LA knees
towards a big white peaky thing
which sticks indignant finger
in the air at this casual abuse:
it was mountain enough for
us: little island racers.

But it wasn't Rainier.
Those sweet Olympians
forswore what we saw was nothing.

O your so big
invisible mountain
meaning **O** to me
without seeing your
O awe.

Cascading
over over-keen eyes
we see a bunch of
hummocks.

Straining high seeking
eyes onto lowlife clouds
cracking
chardonnay with
agitated stun-dance
downing chasers
mildewed entrails
beneath the awnings
outcast smokers
levitated pelts
talking death blue
in the face with a
barrel of
baby rabbit skins.

But Ever Exulted With Bare Necessity
(metal moves me)

alien
giraffe
ina
puny
human hand
arresting
spectacular of metal
languishing in
thrift shop
to pin to
my
lapel
my
to-die-for
long-necked
lash-long
leggy-ah
all-time
big-on
best
word
ever

Can One Seen Beast Be A Wrong One Seen?
(other things move in the eternal intermission)

Tracking
after dark
magic one with
painted face
constellations of
deer eyes puncture
fungal tree-drop.

Zhang Er's
search lights
temperate
rain forest
with bending
backyard
sleuth
four-legged
shadow-beast
moved with
snigger and
total tease.

Never Seeing Raccoon
(I eat its words)

Forepaws

one who lifts things up, they rub, scrub, scratch
they rub and scratch
they take everything in their hands
they touch things, they scratch
they pick up things
graspers
they pick up things, they rub and scratch
one who picks up things
one very clever with its fingers
they handle things, they use hands as a tool
they handle things
graspers
they pick things up, one who touches things
one who rubs, picks up things with hands
washes with hands, they scratch graspers

asban, ah-ra-koon-em
welkol, wilkol, wulkol, wutko
mapachitl, atuki, q'oala's
aasebun, aissibun, shauii
essebanes, wutki, eespan, wtala
wtakalinch, hespan, nachenum, aispan
sha-we, asban, at-cha
aispun essepan, wood-ko shapata
ethepata, swini, que-o-koo
k'alas

Face

painted one, blackened face
blackened face and feet
white bands on face
one with marked face

shiuaa, attigbro
nashi
macheelee, macheelee
cbel'igacocib

80

Magic Thing

magic one with painted face
masked demon spirit
one who makes magic
one with magic, one with magic
one who makes real magic
one with magic
she who talks with spirits
she little old one who knows things
she who watches
witch, spirit

weekah tegalega
gahado-goka-gogosa
macho-on
wee-kah, wee-chah, wee-kahsah, wici, wicha
wee-kah tegalega, wici
mee-kah, mee-chah, mee-kahsa
macca-n-e
wayatcha
see-o-ahtlah-ma-kas-kay
ee-yah-mah-tohn
tsa-ga-gla-tai

Tail

long-tailed bearlike one
those of big-tailed, long-tailed kind
big long tailed ones
ring-tailed one
big long tailed
big-tailed, long-tailed ones

siah-opoots-itswoot
ee-ree-ah-gee
gah-gwah-gee, cah-hee-ah-gway
shinte-gleska
kagh-quau-ga
ee-ree

Doggish

dog, of dog kind
doglike leaper
doglike one
tamed like dog
night doglike one
of the dog kind
doglike leaper

ah-ohn, mayuato
agaua
wacgina, ausup
ah-ohn, ah-oon
agwana

Feeder

graspers of crayfish
doglike leaper on crabs and crayfish
pulls out crayfish with hands
doglike leapers on crabs and crayfish

shauii
mauyato
seip-kuat, siep-mantei
aguara-po-pav

Pure Raccoon

kaka-nostake
guassini, guachini
o'at
ottaguin, ochateguin
tcokda, patkas
kai-kai-yuts
klapissime
va-owok
pilquits
pah-suh-de-na
dEwu'si
roosotto
kanulo-nixa-niso

Part Two

Stella's Dream

And glory, like a phoenix midst her fires,
Exhales her odours, blazes, and expires.

Lord Byron

Stella's Dream
(she danced it with astonished voice)

Stella dreamed a dream
and in that dream she
dreamt her mother's
bedroom overlooked
a yard where perched
three enormous phoenixes
on strange structures
imitating hawks
enormous mega-red
fire or flame or redder.
Desperate to pluck
wide-awake the exact
redness from her
dream.

Their backs turned away
their faces turned away
turned from each other
turned towards the city
in different places.

Listen, *said Stella*,
to us three English poets
who she'd never met:
it was you three!

Us three English poets
stood wrung-out
dwindling and downcast
under New York's
luminous night heights
within reach of a journey's end
caught in a stranger's dream.

Unmythical.
Miniscule.
Unfeathered.
Pinkie, Peaky and Perturbed.

Upstairs in the Gershwin Hotel
my unworn red skirt
flamed along the hem.

Stella shone again:

Not flying – (not sex
Not flying faces – (not wet
Not towards her – (her dream
Towards her city – (not ours

Each in a different place
perched huge and hawk-like
and magnificent.

What a dream to live up
and so dreadful to
be in it for ever
re-
evolving.

(Aside)

Manhattan frosts
steel-toothpick cold-cahoots

?

is it cyclical to
congratulate

?

sublime to
disparage

?

what's that little word

?

at the end of the menu

?

beverage as bloodthirst

?

is it cynical

?

They Gathered Like Cloud-Ragged-Rooks
(to a drum roll on bent spoons)

The three phoenixes
stood hooded hawk-like
behind the lectern
each in the same place
each at a different time:
being in the city they
could not face the city.

Their prehistoric
wings flapped majestic
with melodrama
flinderings under
obdurate silence
pecked into parenthesis.

Having lived so long was a
New World worth dying for?

Is there death after death?

Ornate mind-follies
for the dispirited
coagulating on
outskirts of an
endless orbital
to nowhere
in the fast lane
without song.

A ruffling of feathers flying barwise.

(Aside)

After motionless the
tick comes terrible
awaking the
        audible vocalist
in the next room with
big retribution and
flecks of
        dawn chorus
    banning
hecklers in the
outback.

We all know
what killed
cock robin
desiring
a shade of
desperate
        flaming
redbreast.

The Phoenixes Drink Deep
(stacking mythologies on flindered wings)

The three phoenixes perched against the bar
in a deeply unfashionable gaff
in Manhattan:
six feet under resting in the dark
six eyes whelking in the wrong place
back-dropped with baseball.
Being oh-so-bloody-English
they hankered for the soft
background twitter of cricket
wafting homesick out of India.

Hunched and awkwardly
un-hawkish
furtive words became
their furry quarry.
Being in a dream was not a
good career move
but the only place to be:
a hiding to nothing is
a blessing amongst myths when
perched against a bar
with no particular place to go
in Manhattan.

(Aside)

A spiel of
patter
          claws these
highwire crossedbills
thrumming meekly a
trio of
          off-peak woodpeckers
across the diaphragm
of dead wood and
bored
        conifer
                    faces
pine

        for what

        (?)

One Phoenix Hives Off
(he tried to fly)

He walked up
Broadway
bereft:
got bumped
at JFK
an overnight stay
in
Ramada – he says –
isn't a flaming hot
myth
when you're not living
the dream
but a
splendidly morbid
night
of strewn desolation
and
totally
unreal spaghetti.

devastation in the inauthentic.

(Aside)

The spiritual cashier
scatters ethereal peanuts
to the wind of
reinvention
potshots grow
offshoots
with asses ears.

Dying from too much
afterlife this being
eternal beings
drags a pace
on
tattered wings.

To see constellations
in New York
fly up –
look down
for ever
and a night
is a time to fill
with gazing.

Two Phoenixes Hive Off
(they try to fly)

On our way to JFK
Destiny Rides Again
in the back of
our shared yellow cab:
her unimpeachable
red hair laughing
into mine so close
we are almost related:
supernatural-gingerhood.

'She's a writer'
said the driver
when she'd vanished
'She's Destiny'
he said.

The two phoenixes
bolted upright &
mortice locked
beaks
in inquisition:
who was that
fourth one
a-flaming
besides
us?

Eternity poked a fluke
between
our starked-out eyes.

(Aside)

The grand jury of the mind
shipwrecked
in the centre of this myth.
We fly on a wing and a
mantis dance
mulling over miracles &
sickly smelling air food.

Relentlessly eastwards
in a face-off with the moon
above the Atlantic plastic
cups slop lukewarm tea.

Bouts of light
flirt through
unseen voice
beat urgent hearts
against a worm forest of
frozen girders.

Starring in another's
dream lumbers towards
deadlock.
A head upon
a boulder
is not a head
upon a shoulder.

Home to Roost
(no train today a bus is on its way – get in the queue)

In Sheffield
feathers shed from
ittered clothes and
a bunch of
Arctic Monkeys bought
for a song in
San Francisco echo
Fake Tales
through the kitchen
and we
don't know the distance
we
flew too
far too
damn far.

Hunter's Bar so
near it hurts our
spectral myth-wings.

It is time for ashes.

Stuff the washing machine.

Sleep long. And again.

After-dreams
are elevators
always out-of-order.

(Aside)

I squeeze
a tube of lotion
from the four corners of
my toilet bag
'Kiss My Face'
it says
deliriously
smelling of
Whale
Elk
&
One-who-rubs
with-bands-on
face-masked
demon-spirit-ring
tailed-doglike
leaper-grasper-of
crayfish
kaka-nostake
raccoon

And But Comes To And
(ultimate ember flutter)

The last
dream-phoenix
closes
Melville's
Moby
and
abandons
Abaddon
the hangnail
cracked
from
Adam
but
that
s
another
mandrake
story
after
all
.
.
.
.
.
.
.
.
.
.

Just Another Day

Just Another Day
(A love poem to my love on his birthday)

There is nothing I can say
under the full gaze of
September planets and other eyes ...

everything I tried to write turned to
love and this is not the place to
say such things ...

age is not everything
remotely concerned with sweet
nothings sinking in timeless arms ...

what's another **O** between
you and me. Just another birth of a
another precious day ...

Acknowledgements

Raccoon was first published in 2006 as a Free Poetry publication by Boise State University. I would like to thank Stella for her amazing dream and the telling of it. The indigenous peoples of the Americas for their 'raccoon' words. James Joyce for the half-line lime-lighted in Evergreen. Everyone mentioned in these pages named and unnamed.

Glow in the Darklunar Calendar, July was originally produced as a broadside by Woodland Pattern, Milwaukee under the title *Litha*. All the full moon names in this sequence have been collected from various countries and cultures ancient and modern.

A Nocturnall Upon S. Lucies Day was first published in 2004 by Gargoyle Editions, Sheffield.

Other poems have appeared in the following magazines and journals: *Blackbox Manifold, Dusie, Fascicle, fragmente, In Their Own Words, IsPress, Kaurab, A Tonalist Poetry Feature in Jacket, Noon, Roundyhouse,* and *unarmed.*

Lightning Source UK Ltd.
Milton Keynes UK

178402UK00001B/22/P